Adore the Chc

How to embrace the chaos within an ADHD brain, banish the bullsh*t & discover what works for you. A self-help book by Rachael Beattie, on how to shrink your inner doubts, work around fear and live a happier life.

"If there's someone out there worried about under-achieving, or not feeling, or looking, right to the outside world, I want them to read this book and know they're not alone." says Rachael.

In over a decade of self-employment, Rachael Beattie has had her fair share of ups and downs. These include public struggles, body confidence issues, debilitating anxiety, bipolar disorder and ADHD, or attention deficit hyperactivity disorder, a neurodevelopmental condition characterised by symptoms of inattention, hyperactivity, and impulsivity.

In *Adore the Chaos*, Rachael reveals her darkest moments and those light-bulb ones, plus the hard-won lessons she's learned along the way. She's overcome heartbreak, ended toxic family relationships, and managed her mental health for the better. Her book will help you accept your imperfections, find inner strength, and be true to yourself.

Brave, honest, and insightful, with a generous helping of Rachael's honest Geordie humour, *Adore the Chaos* is an empowering and uplifting guide to finding your personal joy, whatever that might look like.

CONTENTS

Chapter 12
Relaxation: make time for enjoyable activities, hobbies and relaxation.

Chapter 13
Limit distractions: create a workspace with minimal distractions to improve focus and productivity.

Chapter 14
Celebrate small wins: acknowledge and celebrate your achievements, no matter how small.

Chapter 15
Be kind to yourself: practise self-compassion and understand that ADHD is a part of who you are.

ACKNOWLEDGMENTS
To all the people who said I couldn't!

Before learning can happen, you must believe you have the ability to learn. Sadly, many people with ADHD don't. If they have experienced failures, they can develop a fixed mindset and think, *"what's the point? I'll never succeed".*

Since the age of five, and being told to go to school, I just didn't want to go. I don't really understand the reasons behind why I didn't want to go to school. But I just knew I didn't want to go. Was it because I didn't understand what they were trying to teach me? Because I didn't know how to connect and make friends? Or was it too overwhelming?

I just knew that I didn't want to go to school. I remember the days where I used to cry and cry and cry to my mam, saying "I just don't want to go mam".

"But you have to go to school," she replied.

I used to think *why do I have to?*

My mam used to say: "this is where you have to learn", "this is where you connect and make friends", "this is where you grow and learn."

Another day, at the age of thirteen that I remember vividly. Another day of thinking *I've got to get the bus, I've got to be on time, I've got to get dressed. I've got to interact and talk to people.*

I just don't want to!

I am still struggling in the classroom not understanding what the teacher has been talking about.

And that's when I'd actually go to school.

I'd been missing a lot of school during that time. Loads and loads of school, because I just didn't like being there.

I still don't know why I didn't want to be there. Yet again, it's probably because I just didn't feel like I fit in anywhere.

I'll take you on a little adventure back to when I was about fourteen years old. I started to drink on the weekends in the park. Then it went into going out at night.

Still only fourteen years old! However, I loved being part of a world where everyone was going out. They were older. They were around nineteen years old and I had become one of them. I was part of this world where I could be going out, getting in cars with boys, getting dressed up wearing makeup, sneaking out, pretending that I'm sleeping at my friend's house. Instead, I was actually starting to go out with these older people to pubs. I am only fourteen or fifteen years old, but actually, at the time, it unlocked something inside of me.

I would save my dinner money. I wouldn't even eat throughout the week so I could save my money to buy drinks, tabs and bus fare. I would sell my granny to get myself out on a weekend. It was all I lived for. I lived for the fast weekends, the highs, and the blowout music, the getting dressed up, the sneaking about, the connecting with boys via texts - It was just so exciting. My brain felt really, really happy, extremely happy.

I was using the alcohol as a confidence boost. This was my thing, it really made me feel like I was unstoppable. I felt like I could dance, I could laugh, I could sing and I could be happy. Different, happy.

Then at about sixteen years old I started to think, *"right that's it!"*
I'm not going to school anymore. So I left school with no GCSEs. I left school thinking I was a failure, that I couldn't do the things that I was told I should be doing at that age.

I decided that I wanted to be in this grown-up world, so I went and started to be in the adult world of college. I took myself to our local college, I knew this would be the start of me building my qualifications. Having no GCSE's I started at the lower level of ICT but before I knew it I was moved by my tutor to the advanced studies which has never ever happened to me before! College was the place that really helped me to grow. But I was still living for the weekends, using alcohol to be that boost of confidence. However, before long that turned into Wednesday night, Thursday night, Friday night, as well as the weekend, and using alcohol to get through the days and focus on something exciting.

What I'm realising now, is that actually my brain needs that excitement to feel happy.

Now at an older age, and being diagnosed with ADHD, I know that my brain needs stimulation to be happy.
I know that stimulation can come in many different forms. Now I'm able to understand more and find the right coping strategies. Things like going to the gym, for a walk, or a run. These were the things that I used to help recover from my alcohol addiction. It was my new confidence boost.

The alcohol, at the time, was the thing that I used to let me talk to people, to understand, and really let my brain do its thing. But now, being older, I no longer use alcohol to change my mood.

It's great to be able to say that really. It's such a proud moment.

There were days where all that mattered was alcohol and food, The binge eating was out of control because when you eat chocolate and sugary things in this way, it hits our brains with dopamine. I now know my brain needs lots of dopamine and serotonin to make me feel happy.

The things that I find really help my confidence and coping, are strategies like exercise, along with talking therapies, yoga, walking and cold-water therapy. Walking the dogs, seeing friends, going for coffee, dancing in the kitchen, asking for help. It all helps and makes a difference

Having an ADHD diagnosis and knowing that it means I have a neurodivergent brain, I now feel my brain is awesome, my brain is amazing.
My brain works amazingly now, but back when I was twelve years old I thought I was sick, stupid, that I couldn't do it,that I was broken.

But actually, we are unstoppable.

Lots of love.

Rachael Beattie

Chapter 1

Before we start, I want to share something. I don't have life all sussed out. Neither does that person down the road with the perfect makeup and Instagram living room, so cut yourself some slack!

Routine and structure

Establishing a daily routine with set times for tasks and breaks will reduce stress and improve overall productivity and well-being. Here's a template to help you establish a structured daily routine:

Morning routine:

1. Wake up: set a specific time to wake up each day, allowing for 7-9 hours of sleep.

2. Morning hygiene: pay attention to personal hygiene, including brushing teeth, showering, and getting dressed.

3. Breakfast: fuel your body with a healthy breakfast.

4. Mindfulness or meditation: spend a few minutes in quiet reflection, mindfulness, or meditation to centre yourself for the day ahead.

5. Exercise: engage in physical activity, whether it's a morning walk, yoga, or a workout, to boost your energy and mood.

Work/study time:

6. Task planning: start your work or study session by outlining your goals for the day

7. Focused work/study blocks: allocate specific time blocks (e.g. 90 minutes) for focused work or study, and avoid distractions during these periods.

8. Short breaks: take short breaks (5-10 minutes) between work/study blocks to stretch, hydrate, or relax briefly.

9. Lunch: have a healthy lunch at a consistent time.

Afternoon routine:

10. More work/study: continue with your work or study tasks, keeping to your planned schedule.

11. Meetings/appointments: schedule meetings, appointments, or group activities during this part of the day.

12. Afternoon break: take a longer break (20-30 minutes) to recharge, and consider a walk or a healthy snack.

Evening routine:

13. Wrap up work/study: complete any remaining tasks and make a to-do list for the next day.

14. Dinner: enjoy a balanced meal for dinner at a consistent time.

15. Relaxation: engage in activities that help you relax and unwind, like reading, hobbies, or spending quality time with family.

16. Screen-free time: limit screen time, especially from phones and computers, at least an hour before bedtime.

Night routine:

17. Prep for tomorrow: lay out clothes, pack bags, and ensure everything is ready for the next day.

18. Wind down: spend some time winding down, with gentle stretching, journaling, or practising gratitude.

19. Bedtime: set a regular bedtime that allows for sufficient sleep.

General tips:

1. Prioritise tasks: focus on the most important and time-sensitive tasks during your peak energy hours.

2. Be flexible: while routine is beneficial, allow for some flexibility to adapt to unexpected events.

3. Limit multitasking: concentrate on one task at a time to boost efficiency and reduce stress.

4. Stay hydrated: drink enough water throughout the day to maintain your energy levels.

5. Practise self-care: make time for activities that promote mental and emotional well-being, like spending time with loved ones, or hobbies.

6. Review and adjust: periodically assess your routine and make adjustments to improve its effectiveness and suit your evolving needs.

Remember that creating a routine is a personal process, so tailor it to your specific goals and lifestyle. Consistency and commitment are key to reducing stress and enhancing your daily life.

Brain dump space

Brain dump space

Chapter 2

Prioritising

Use to-do lists to prioritise, and focus on, completing one task at a time rather than getting overwhelmed by many.

Prioritising tasks and using to-do lists is an effective way to get, and stay, organised and be more productive. Here's a step-by-step guide on how to prioritise tasks and focus on completing them one at a time:

1. Create a to-do list:
Start by listing all the tasks you need to accomplish. This could include work-related tasks, personal chores, and other responsibilities. Use a digital tool, a physical notepad, or a task management app to create your list.

2. Break down large tasks:
If you have large or complex tasks on your list, break them down into smaller, more manageable sub-tasks. This makes them easier to tackle one step at a time.

3. Set deadlines:
Assign deadlines to each task or sub-task. This creates a sense of urgency and keeps you on track. Be realistic with deadlines or you'll set yourself up for failure.

4. Assess priorities:
Determine the importance and urgency of each task. Use a system like the Eisenhower Matrix to categorise tasks into four quadrants.
- Urgent and important: do these tasks first.
- Important but not urgent: schedule these tasks for later.
- Urgent but not important: delegate these tasks if possible.
- Not urgent and not important: consider eliminating or postponing these tasks.

5. Prioritise your list:
Order your tasks based on their priority. Focus on completing high-priority tasks before moving on to lower-priority ones. This way, you'll be addressing the most critical items first.

6. Eliminate distractions:
Find a quiet, comfortable workspace. Turn off device notifications, close unnecessary tabs or apps, and let others know you're in a focused work mode. Minimising distractions will help you concentrate on one task at a time.

7. Use time blocks:
Allocate specific time blocks for each task. For example, you might work on a high-priority task for 60 minutes, take a short break, and then move on to the next task. This technique, known as time blocking, can enhance your productivity.

8. Focus on one task at a time:
Avoid multitasking, as it can decrease your efficiency and quality of work. Concentrate on completing the task at hand before moving on to the next one.

9. Track your progress:
As you complete tasks, cross them off your to-do list. This provides a sense of accomplishment and helps you stay motivated.

10. Adapt and review:
Throughout the day, be flexible and open to adjusting your priorities if unexpected tasks or emergencies arise. After completing your tasks, or at the end of the day, review your list and plan for tomorrow.

Remember, effective task prioritisation and time management take practice. It's important to find a system that works best for you. Equally important is to refine your approach to improve productivity and reduce overwhelm.

Brain dump space

Brain dump space

Chapter 3

Take smaller steps

Breaking tasks into smaller steps is a practical strategy to increase productivity and manage complex or overwhelming projects.

Follow these steps to do it effectively:

1. Identify the task:
Clearly define the task you need to accomplish. Be specific about the end goal so you can break it down effectively.

2. List sub-tasks:
Break the task into smaller, more manageable sub-tasks. These must be actions that contribute to the overall goal. List all the necessary steps.

3. Prioritise sub-tasks:
Determine which sub-tasks are most critical, or need to be completed first. Consider dependencies because some sub-tasks may rely on others.

4. Set deadlines:
Assign deadlines to each sub-task. Having timeframes will help you to stay on track and allocate your time efficiently.

5. Allocate resources:
Identify the resources (materials, tools, people) you need for each sub-task. Make sure you have everything in place before you begin.

6. Create a to-do list:
Gather the sub-tasks, their deadlines, and resource requirements into a to-do list or project plan. Tools like task management apps or a simple paper list can be helpful.

7. Start with the first sub-task:
Begin working on the first sub-task according to your plan. Focus on completing it before moving on to the next.

8. Track progress:

Regularly review your progress. Mark off completed sub-tasks and assess how well you're adhering to your timeline.

9. Adjust as necessary:

If you encounter unexpected challenges or changes, be flexible in adjusting your plan. Modify deadlines, allocate additional resources, or revise sub-tasks if required.

10. Celebrate milestones:

Acknowledge your achievements along the way. Celebrating small victories can help boost motivation and morale.

11. Maintain focus:

Concentrate on the current sub-task rather than worrying about the entire project. This avoids overwhelm.

12. Seek help:

If you're struggling with a particular sub-task, don't hesitate to ask for assistance or seek advice from colleagues, mentors or experts.

13. Review and reflect:

Once the entire task is complete, take time to reflect on the process. Consider what went well and what could be improved for the future.

Dividing tasks into smaller steps not only makes them less daunting, but also enhances your ability to plan, execute, and track progress. This is a valuable technique to improve productivity. This way, you'll be able to achieve your goals more efficiently.

Brain dump space

Brain dump space

Chapter Four

Time management

Use timers or apps to manage your time and stay on track. This way, you'll stay organised, maintain focus on tasks, and generally increase productivity.

Here are some tips on how to effectively use timers and apps for time management:

1. Identify your priorities:
Before you start using timers or apps, determine your top priorities and tasks for the day. This will help you allocate your time effectively.

2. Choose the right tools:
Select timers or apps that align with your needs and preferences. There are various options available, from simple kitchen timers to sophisticated time management apps. Some popular apps include Todoist, Trello, Asana, and Toggl.

3. Set specific goals:
Define clear goals for each task or activity on which you plan to work. Having a specific objective will make it easier to allocate the right amount of time.

4. The Pomodoro Technique:
Consider using the Pomodoro Technique, which involves working for a set period (typically 25 minutes), followed by a short break. Timer apps like PomoDone can help you implement this process effectively.

5. Time blocking:
Allocate specific time blocks for different activities or projects. Use timers to stay disciplined within these blocks and avoid distractions.

6. Task lists and reminders:

Use apps that allow you to create task lists and set reminders. This can help you stay organised and ensure you don't forget important tasks.

7. Prioritise and batch tasks:

Group similar tasks together and tackle them during dedicated time blocks. Prioritise high-value tasks to accomplish your most important goals.

8. Limit distractions:

Set a timer for short periods to focus exclusively on a task, and during that time, turn off notifications, put your phone on silent, and close unnecessary tabs on your computer.

9. Review and adjust:

Regularly review your time management approach and make adjustments as needed. If you find that a particular app or technique isn't working for you, don't hesitate to try something else.

10. Analyse your data:

Many time management apps offer features to track how you spend your time. Analyse this data to identify patterns and areas for improvement in your time management habits.

11. Be realistic:

When setting timers or scheduling tasks, be realistic about how much time each activity will take. Overestimating or underestimating leads to frustration and inefficiency.

12. Maintain balance:

Remember to allocate time for breaks, leisure activities, and self-care. Overworking can lead to burnout, so strike a balance between work and well-being.

13. Stay consistent:

Consistency is key to effective time management. Stick to your chosen methods and tools to establish good time management habits.

14. Seek accountability:

Share your time management goals with a friend, colleague, or mentor who can hold you accountable.

By using timers and apps strategically, you can optimise your time, increase productivity, and reduce stress in your daily life. Experiment with different techniques and tools to find what works best for you, and remember that effective time management is a skill that improves with practice.

Brain dump space

Brain dump space

Chapter Five

Self care

Make self-care a priority. Get enough sleep, eat well, exercise regularly, and practise relaxation techniques. Self-care is crucial to maintaining physical and mental health. Making self-care a priority greatly improves the overall quality of life.

Here are some tips on how to incorporate self-care into your daily routine:

1. **Prioritise sleep:**
   Aim for 7-9 hours of quality sleep each night. Create a bedtime routine that helps you relax, such as reading a book or taking a warm bath. Avoid screens and caffeine close to bedtime.

2. **Eat well:**
   Fuel your body with a balanced diet that includes plenty of fruit, vegetables, lean proteins, and whole grains. Stay hydrated by drinking enough water throughout the day.

3. **Regular exercise:**
   Incorporate regular physical activity into your routine. Find a form of exercise that you enjoy, whether it's jogging, yoga, dancing, or simply taking a brisk walk. Exercise not only improves physical health but also releases endorphins to boost your mood.

4. **Practice relaxation techniques:**
   Stress management is key to self-care. Try relaxation techniques like deep breathing, meditation, or mindfulness to reduce stress and anxiety. These practices help you remain calm and focused.

5. **Set boundaries:**
   Learn to say no when necessary. Overcommitting leads to burnout. Setting boundaries and effective time management are essential for self-care.

6. **Social connections:**
   Maintain relationships with family and friends. Social support is vital for emotional well-being. Make time to connect with loved ones, through phone calls, video chats, or face-to-face get-togethers.

7. **Hobbies and leisure activities:**
   Engage in activities you love, and that bring you joy. Whether it's painting, playing an instrument, gardening, or any other hobby, you'll find it rejuvenating to dedicate time to things about which you are passionate.

8. **Unplug:**
   Take breaks from technology and screens. Constant exposure to screens contributes to stress and disrupts your sleep. Set aside tech-free time to relax and unwind.

9. **Self-reflection:**
   Spend time reflecting on your feelings and thoughts. Journaling is a valuable tool for self-discovery and emotional processing.

10. **Professional help:**
    Seek professional help if you're struggling with your mental health. Therapists, counsellors, and healthcare professionals will provide support and guidance when needed.

11. **Self-compassion:**
    Be kind and forgiving to yourself. Treat yourself with the same level of care and compassion you would offer to a friend. Avoid self-criticism and negative self-talk.

12. **Regular checkups:**
    Schedule regular checkups with your healthcare provider to monitor your physical health and promptly address any concerns.

Self-care is not selfish. It's essential for your overall well-being. By making self-care a priority and incorporating well-being practices into your daily life, you will manage stress better, maintain good health, and lead a more fulfilling life.

Brain dump space

Brain dump space

Chapter Six

Mindfulness and meditation

Mindfulness techniques help you stay present and reduce anxiety, while meditation improves focus. These are powerful practices with a positive impact on mental well-being and overall quality of life.

Let's take a closer look at both concepts and how they'll benefit you:

Mindfulness:

1. **Staying present:**
   Mindfulness is being fully present, in the moment, while paying attention to your thoughts, feelings, and sensations without judgement. It increases awareness of your surroundings, and the actual, present moment, rather than dwelling on the past or worrying about the future.

2. **Reducing anxiety:**
   Mindfulness is an effective tool for managing anxiety. By focusing on the here and now, the cycle of anxious thoughts is broken, and physical symptoms of anxiety, such as increased heart rate and shallow breathing, are reduced.

3. **Enhancing emotional regulation:**
   Mindfulness increases awareness of emotions as they arise. This awareness allows you to respond in a more balanced and constructive way, rather than reacting impulsively.

4. **Improving relationships:**
   Practising mindfulness leads to better communication and more empathetic interactions with others. By being fully present and attentive, your connections and understanding of people are deepened.

Meditation:

1. **Improved focus and concentration:**
   Meditation involves training your mind to focus on a single point of attention, such as your breath or a mantra. Over time, this enhances your ability to concentrate on tasks and reduce distractions.

2. **Stress Reduction:**
   Meditation is known for its stress-reducing benefits. Regular practice triggers the relaxation response in your body, lowering stress hormones and promoting a sense of calm and well-being.

3. **Enhanced self-awareness:**
   Meditation increases self-awareness by encouraging introspection and self-reflection.
   This leads to personal growth and a deeper self-understanding.

4. **Better sleep:**
   Many people find that meditation improves sleep quality. It relaxes the body and quietens the mind, making it easier to fall asleep and stay asleep.

5. **Pain management:**
   Meditation is also used as a complementary approach for managing chronic pain. It changes the way pain is perceived and improves pain tolerance.

   It's important to note that mindfulness and meditation are skills that require practice. Consistency is key to experiencing their full benefits.

   Start with short sessions and gradually increase the duration as you become more comfortable. There are a number of meditation and mindfulness practices, so take time to explore different techniques to find what works best for you.

   Whether you're looking to reduce anxiety, enhance focus, or improve your overall well-being, incorporating mindfulness and meditation into your daily routine is a valuable step toward achieving those goals.

Brain dump space

Brain dump space

Chapter Seven

Realistic goals

Be realistic about what you can achieve in a day. Don't overcommit. Setting realistic goals is a crucial aspect of effective time management and productivity, and helps to avoid stress, burnout, and a sense of failure.

Here are some ideas on how to set realistic goals:

1. Prioritise:
Start by identifying your most important tasks and goals. Focus on the high-impact activities that will make the most significant difference to your life or work.

2. Break it down:
If you have a big goal, break it down into small, manageable tasks or steps. The goal will feel less daunting and you'll be able to track progress effectively.

3. Assess your capacity:
Take an honest look at your available time. Assess your energy levels. Consider commitments, like work, family, and personal time. Ensure your goals align with your current capacity.

4. Set specific goals:
Instead of vague goals like 'work on a project,' be specific about what you want to accomplish. For example, 'complete the first draft of the project report' is a more precise goal.

5. Use the SMART criteria:
SMART stands for Specific, Measurable, Achievable, Relevant, and Time-bound. Applying these criteria to your goal ensures they are realistic. Ask yourself if your goal meets these criteria.

6. Consider your past performance:
Reflect on your previous achievements and how long similar tasks or goals have taken in the past. This provides valuable insights with regard to realistic expectations.

7. Set limits:
Don't overload your to-do list. Limit the number of goals you set for the day, so the list is manageable. Make sure you have enough time and focus for each goal.

8. Be flexible:
Life is unpredictable, so be ready to adjust your goals if unexpected events or priorities arise during the day. It's okay to adapt and re-prioritise as needed.

9. Review and adjust:
Regularly review your goals and your progress. If you find that you're often unable to accomplish what you've set out to do, think about adjusting expectations or re-evaluating priorities.

10. Learn to say no:
It's essential to recognise your limits. Don't overcommit. Politely decline anything that you genuinely cannot accommodate without compromising your well-being or the quality of your work.

Remember, setting realistic goals is about finding the balance between challenging yourself and ensuring your goals are achievable within your current circumstances. This approach leads to increased productivity, reduced stress, and a greater sense of accomplishment.

Brain dump space

Brain dump space

Chapter Eight

Saying no

Avoid overloading yourself with commitments. It's okay to say no. Learning to say no is an important skill to help avoid overload and maintain a healthy work-life balance.

Some tips on how to say no:

1. Be clear and direct:
When you need to decline a request, do so in a clear and direct manner. Don't beat around the bush or offer vague excuses. Instead, express your decision firmly but politely.

2. Prioritise your time:
Before agreeing to a new commitment, assess your current workload and personal obligations. Make sure you understand your priorities clearly so you can make informed decisions about what to take on and what to decline.

3. Use 'I' statements:
When saying no, use 'I' statements to communicate your decision. For example, say, 'I can't commit to this right now', or 'I need to focus on other priorities at the moment'. This makes it about your own limitations rather than blaming or criticising the requester.

4. Offer an alternative:
If you genuinely want to help but can't commit, consider offering an alternative solution. For example, you might say, 'I can't do this project, but I can connect you with someone who might be able to help', or 'I can help, but it will have to be at a later date.'

5. Practice saying no:
Saying no is often challenging, especially if you're not used to it. Practice with a friend or in front of a mirror to get comfortable with the words and tone you want to use.

6. Set boundaries:

Establishing clear boundaries for yourself is crucial. Know your limits and communicate them to others. This will prevent you from taking on too much in the first place.

7. Learn to manage guilt:

It's normal to feel guilty when saying no, but remember it's okay to prioritise your well-being and commitments. Don't let guilt dictate your decisions.

8. Buy time:

If you're unsure about a request, don't feel pressured to give an immediate answer. You can say something like, 'Let me check my schedule and get back to you,' which gives you time to evaluate the request.

9. Be consistent:

Once you've established your boundaries and learned to say no, be consistent in your responses. People will come to respect your decisions when they see that you stick to them.

10.Focus on self-care:

Saying no is an essential aspect of self-care. Overcommitting leads to burnout and a negative impact on your well-being. Prioritise your health and happiness by knowing when to say no.

Incorporating these strategies into your life will help you say no, when necessary, without feeling overwhelmed or guilty. It's an important skill that allows you to protect your time and energy for the things that matter most.

Brain dump space

Brain dump space

Chapter Nine

Seek support

Reach out to friends, family, or support groups who understand your challenges. Seeking support is an important step towards coping with life's difficulties. Whichever problem you're facing, family, friends, and groups can be incredibly beneficial.

Here's why and how to seek support

1. Emotional support:
Family and friends can be empathetic, good listeners and understand what you're going through in tough times. They provide a safe space for you to express your feelings and thoughts.
Support groups expose you to people experiencing similar challenges, enabling you to connect with others who truly understand your experiences. These groups often provide a sense of belonging and camaraderie.

2. Practical assistance:
Family and friends, in addition to emotional support, can offer practical help like running errands, providing transport, or assisting with challenging tasks.
Support groups can also offer practical advice and resources related to specific challenges you might be facing, including health issues, addiction concerns, or other life stressors.

3. Reducing isolation:
Sharing your struggles with others combats feelings of loneliness and isolation. Knowing that you're not alone in your experiences provides comfort and a sense of community.

4. Gaining perspective:
Talking to others offers different perspectives and insights into your situation. This lets you see challenges from new angles and can help you discover solutions or coping strategies you hadn't considered.

5. Emotional resilience:

Receiving support bolsters your emotional resilience, making it easier to navigate difficult times. Knowing you have a network of people who care about you boosts your mental and emotional well-being.

How to get support:

- Consider who, in your network, you feel comfortable confiding in. It could be a close friend, family member, or a support group related to your specific challenge.
- Clearly express your need for support. Communicate what you're going through and the type of assistance or emotional support you require.
- Share your thoughts and feelings openly and honestly. Authenticity fosters deeper connections and more meaningful support.
- While seeking support is important, it's also crucial to set boundaries to ensure your well-being. Let others know what you're comfortable discussing and when.
- Sometimes, seeking the assistance of a therapist, counsellor, or mental health professional is necessary for guidance and support tailored to your needs.

Seeking support is a sign of strength, not weakness. It's vital in managing challenges and improving overall well-being. Don't hesitate to lean on your support network when required, and be willing to reciprocate and support others when they, in turn, are facing difficulties.

Brain dump space

Brain dump space

Chapter Ten

Professional help

Consider working with a therapist or counsellor who specialises in ADHD, and who can provide coping strategies and support. Seeking professional help is an excellent way forward for people dealing with ADHD-related challenges, given that these professionals offer valuable guidance tailored to specific needs.

Here are some key reasons why working with an ADHD specialist can be beneficial:

1. Specialised knowledge:
ADHD specialists have in-depth knowledge and understanding of the intricacies of ADHD. They are well-versed in the latest research, diagnostic criteria, and treatment options, ensuring you receive accurate information and appropriate strategies.

2. Individualised treatment plans:
ADHD is a complex and highly individualised condition. A specialist assesses your unique strengths and challenges and develops a personalised treatment plan to include therapy, medication, or a combination of both.

3. Coping strategies:
ADHD specialists teach effective coping strategies to help you manage symptoms like impulsivity, inattention and hyperactivity. These strategies are valuable in daily life, both personally and professionally.

4. Emotional support:
Living with ADHD can be emotionally challenging, leading to feelings of frustration, low self-esteem and anxiety. Therapists and counsellors provide a safe and non-judgmental space to discuss your feelings and work through emotional issues.

5. Medication management:

If medication is part of your treatment plan, an ADHD specialist can monitor its effectiveness, adjust dosages if necessary, and help you manage any side effects.

6. Skill development:

ADHD specialists help you develop important life skills like time management, organisation and problem-solving, often areas of difficulty for individuals with ADHD.

7. Education and psycho-education:

These provide valuable information about ADHD, helping you better understand the condition and its impact on your life. Psycho-education can be especially helpful to you and your loved ones.

8. Family and relationship support:

ADHD affects not only the individual but also their family and other relationships. A specialist provides guidance on managing ADHD-related challenges in these areas.

9. Goal setting and achievement:

Setting and achieving goals can be challenging for individuals with ADHD. A therapist assists you in setting realistic goals and developing strategies to accomplish them.

10. Long-term support:

ADHD is a lifelong condition, and working with a specialist can provide ongoing support and assistance as you navigate the different stages of your life.

Remember, finding the right therapist or counsellor is essential. Look for professionals who have experience and training in ADHD, and don't hesitate to schedule initial consultations with different providers to find the one that best suits your needs and preferences. Additionally, involving your family or support network in your treatment journey can also help to understand and manage ADHD effectively.

Brain dump space

Brain dump space

Chapter Eleven

Medication

If prescribed by a healthcare professional, medication can be a valuable component of a comprehensive treatment programme for ADHD. Medication helps manage ADHD symptoms, which can in turn reduce burnout

Medications for ADHD are typically divided into two main categories:

1. Stimulant medications:

These are the most commonly prescribed medications for ADHD and include drugs like methylphenidate (e.g. Ritalin), and amphetamine-based medications (e.g. Adderall). They are formulated to improve attention, focus, and impulse control, are often the first line of treatment, and can have rapid and noticeable effects.

2. Non-stimulant medications:

Non-stimulant medications like atomoxetine (e.g. Strattera), guanfacine (e.g. Intuniv), and clonidine (e.g. Kapvay) are also used to treat ADHD. These may be preferred in cases where stimulants are not well-tolerated or if there is concern about potential misuse.

Medications for ADHD are not a cure, but they can help manage symptoms effectively. When used as part of a comprehensive treatment plan, which may also include behavioural therapy, counselling, and lifestyle modifications, medication can improve an individual's ability to focus, control impulses, and better manage daily life. This, in turn, can reduce the risk of burnout by helping individuals with ADHD to navigate their daily tasks and responsibilities more effectively.

It's important to note that medication should always be prescribed and monitored by a qualified healthcare professional, such as a psychiatrist or paediatrician, who specialises in ADHD treatment. This way, the medication choice and dosage are tailored to the individual's specific needs, and monitored for any potential side effects or adjustments necessary. Medication should be used in conjunction with other therapeutic strategies for the most comprehensive and effective treatment of ADHD.

Brain dump space

Brain dump space

Chapter Twelve

Relaxation

Make time for activities you enjoy and that help you relax. This is essential for a balanced and fulfilled life. Hobbies provide an opportunity to unwind, relieve stress, and explore your interests.

Here are some tips on how to make time for these:

1. Prioritise your schedule:
Set aside specific blocks of time for your hobbies just as you would for work or other commitments. Treat this time as non-negotiable.

2. Time management:
Efficiently manage your time by creating a daily or weekly schedule. Allocate slots for your hobbies and stick to them as closely as possible.

3. Set goals:
Establish clear goals for your hobbies. Whether it's learning a new skill or completing a project, having goals motivates you to make time for your hobbies.

4. Limit screen time:
Reduce the time spent on activities like watching TV, scrolling through social media, or playing video games. Use that time for your hobbies instead.

5. Combine activities:
Find ways to incorporate your hobbies into your daily routine. For example, if you enjoy reading, you can read during your commute or while waiting for appointments.

6. Involve others:
Share your hobbies with family and friends. This can turn your hobbies into social activities and make it easier to commit time to them.

7. Set boundaries:
Learn to say no. Sometimes, you have to decline other commitments to make time for your hobbies.

8. Multitasking:
If possible, combine your hobbies with other activities. For instance, if you like painting, you can listen to audiobooks or podcasts related to your interests while you paint.

9. Delegate and outsource:
If your schedule is tight, consider outsourcing tasks like cleaning or grocery shopping to free up more time for your hobbies.

10.Self-care:
Remember, taking time for yourself and your hobbies is a form of self-care. It boosts your mental and emotional well-being, leading to greater productivity in other areas of life.

11. Plan ahead:
Plan activities in advance. Knowing what you want to do during your hobby time can make it easier to commit.

12.Flexibility:
Be flexible with your hobby time. There will be days when unexpected events occur, and you can't engage in your hobbies as planned. Don't stress. Adjust your schedule and make up for it later.

Making time for hobbies is a necessity for maintaining a healthy work-life balance and overall well-being. Prioritise your interests and find joy in pursuing your passions.

Brain dump space

Brain dump space

Chapter Thirteen

Limit Distractions

Create a workspace with minimal distractions to improve focus and productivity. This is essential for improving focus and productivity.

Here are some steps you can take to limit distractions and create an optimal work environment:

1. Dedicated workspace:
Designate a specific area for work, if possible. It could be a separate room, a corner of a room, or even a well-organised desk. Make sure it's primarily used for work to mentally associate it with productivity.

2. Organise and declutter:
Keep your workspace organised and clutter-free. A cluttered desk is distracting and it's often difficult to find what you need. Use shelves, drawers, and organisers to keep everything in its place.

3. Minimise visual distractions:
Choose a plain colour scheme for your workspace. Remove any unnecessary decorations or items that may catch your eye. Use a screensaver or wallpaper that promotes concentration or displays your to-do list.

4. Control noise:
Use noise-cancelling headphones or earplugs to block out background noise. Play instrumental music or white noise if it helps you concentrate. Consider a white noise machine or app if your workspace is in a noisy environment.

5. Set boundaries:
Inform family members or roommates of your work hours to minimise interruptions. Use a 'do not disturb' sign or a digital status indicator to signal when you're working and shouldn't be disturbed.

6. Digital distractions:
Turn off non-essential notifications on your computer and phone. Use website blockers or apps that limit access to distracting websites or social media during work hours. Consider using productivity tools and apps designed to keep you focused.

7. Ergonomics:
Invest in an ergonomic chair and desk setup to ensure comfort during long work hours. Position your computer monitor at eye level to reduce strain on your neck and back.

8. Personalise your space:
While minimalism is important, adding a few personal touches makes your workspace more inviting. Plants, artwork, or motivational quotes improve mood and productivity.

9. Task management:
Keep a to-do list or use a task management app to stay organised and on track. Prioritise tasks and break them into smaller, manageable steps.

10. Regular breaks:
Schedule short breaks during your work day to recharge. Use techniques like the Pomodoro Technique (25 minutes of work followed by a 5-minute break) to maintain focus.

11. Mindfulness and meditation:
Incorporate mindfulness practices or short meditation sessions into your daily routine to improve concentration and reduce stress.

12. Proper lighting:
Ensure your workspace is well-lit to reduce eye strain. Natural light is ideal, but if that's not possible, use task lighting with adjustable brightness.

13. Boundaries for work and leisure:
Maintain clear boundaries between work and leisure. When your work hours are over, close your workspace and engage in non-work activities to recharge.

Creating an ideal workspace may take some experimentation. What works best for one person may not work for another, so adapt these suggestions to suit your preferences and needs. Regularly assess your workspace and make necessary adjustments to maintain a productive and distraction-free environment.

Brain dump space

Brain dump space

Chapter Fourteen

Celebrate small wins

Acknowledge and celebrate your achievements, no matter how small they seem. Celebrating small wins is a powerful practice with a significant positive impact on motivation, well-being, and overall productivity.

Here's why it's important:

1. Boosts motivation:
Recognising and celebrating small achievements boosts motivation to keep working toward your goals. It provides a sense of progress and accomplishment, which is a great source of encouragement.

2. Builds confidence:
Each small win adds to your confidence, making you more likely to tackle bigger challenges. Over time, these incremental victories lead to significant accomplishments.

3. Reduces stress:
Celebrating small wins reduces stress and anxiety by shifting the focus from what you haven't achieved to what you have achieved. It maintains a positive perspective.

4. Cultivates positivity:
Focusing on the positive aspects of your journey fosters a positive mindset. This improves overall well-being and makes the process of achieving your goals more enjoyable.

Here's how to celebrate small wins effectively:

1. Acknowledge them:
Don't dismiss or downplay your small achievements. Recognise them as steps toward your larger goals.

2. Keep a journal:
Maintain a journal to record daily or weekly wins, no matter how insignificant they seem. Reviewing these entries will remind you of progress over time.

3. Share with others:
Celebrate with friends, family or colleagues who support your goals. Sharing wins enhances the joy and motivation you derive from them.

4. Reward yourself:
Treat yourself to something special when you achieve a milestone, even if it's small. It could be as simple as taking a day off, enjoying a favourite meal, or buying yourself a small gift.

5. Set new goals:
After celebrating a small win, set new, slightly more challenging goals to keep the momentum going. This ensures continual progress.

6. Reflect and learn:
Take a moment to reflect on what led to your success. What strategies or actions were effective? Learning from small wins helps replicate success in the future.

7. Visualise the bigger picture:
Remember that each small win is a piece of the puzzle, contributing to your long-term success. Visualise how these small wins will lead you to your ultimate goals.

The journey to achieving your goals is often filled with many small steps. By celebrating small wins, you not only stay motivated and positive but also increase your chances of reaching larger objectives.

Brain dump space

Brain dump space

Chapter Fifteen

Be kind to yourself

Understand that ADHD is a part of who you are, and it's okay to have challenging days. Practice self-compassion. This is crucial when you have ADHD or any other condition that makes life challenging at times.

Some ways to be kind to yourself:

1. Acknowledge your challenges:
Understand that ADHD is a neurobiological condition, not a character flaw. Recognise that it can make certain tasks or situations more difficult for you, and that's okay.

2. Set realistic expectations:
Don't be too hard on yourself when things don't go as planned. Set achievable goals and break tasks into smaller, manageable steps. Celebrate your small victories along the way.

3. Forgive yourself:
If you make mistakes or forget things, remember that it happens to everyone, not just those with ADHD. Be forgiving and remind yourself that mistakes are opportunities for growth.

4. Practice mindfulness:
Mindfulness and meditation keep you in the present moment, reduce the overwhelm that often accompanies ADHD, and foster self-awareness and self-compassion.

5. Seek support:
Don't hesitate to reach out to friends, family, or a therapist for support. Talking to someone who understands your struggles provides emotional relief and helpful advice.

6. Use ADHD-friendly strategies:
Explore strategies and tools that work for you. This might include setting up routines, using task lists, or employing time management techniques. Finding what works best for you can significantly reduce daily challenges.

7. Educate yourself:

Learning more about ADHD empowers you to better understand your strengths and weaknesses. Knowledge is a powerful tool in the journey to self-compassion.

8. Celebrate your strengths:

ADHD frequently comes with unique strengths like creativity, hyperfocus, and enthusiasm. Celebrate these strengths and use them to your advantage.

9. Take breaks:

Recognise when you need a break and allow yourself to step away from tasks that are causing frustration or stress. Taking short breaks can actually boost productivity and help you recharge.

10.It's a journey:

Healing, growth, and self-compassion are ongoing processes. Understand that there will be good days and challenging days, and that's part of your unique journey.

Always remember, you're not alone, and there are many resources and supportive communities available for individuals with ADHD. Being kind to yourself and practising self-compassion are important steps in managing ADHD effectively and living a fulfilled life.

Summary

Managing ADHD burnout is an ongoing process, and what works for one person may not work for another. Experiment with these strategies and tailor them to your specific needs and preferences. It's perfectly normal to have ups and downs when managing ADHD. Be patient with yourself, and don't hesitate to seek professional guidance if you find it challenging to cope with burnout, or if your symptoms significantly impact your daily life. Your healthcare provider can tailor a treatment plan that best suits your unique needs.

About the author

My name is Rachael Beattie, ADHD cheerleader and the founder of the Neuro Boost Business Community Hub. Come with me on a journey to create accessible Neuro Boost support hubs across the UK, offering mental health, well-being, funding and financial support, plus ADHD and or Autism assessments.

www.neuroboost.info

Love Rachael xxx

Brain dump space

Brain dump space

Brain dump space

Brain dump space

Brain dump space

Brain dump space

Brain dump space

Brain dump space

Brain dump space

Printed in Great Britain
by Amazon